50 Gourmet International Dishes

By: Kelly Johnson

Table of Contents

- Coq au Vin (France)
- Paella Valenciana (Spain)
- Beef Wellington (United Kingdom)
- Chicken Tikka Masala (India)
- Szechuan Pork (China)
- Sushi Rolls (Japan)
- Osso Buco (Italy)
- Moussaka (Greece)
- Korean Bibimbap (Korea)
- Moroccan Tagine (Morocco)
- Thai Green Curry (Thailand)
- Turkish Manti (Turkey)
- Swedish Meatballs (Sweden)
- Brazilian Feijoada (Brazil)
- Ethiopian Doro Wat (Ethiopia)
- Mexican Mole Poblano (Mexico)
- Russian Beef Stroganoff (Russia)
- German Sauerbraten (Germany)
- Argentinian Asado (Argentina)
- Lebanese Kibbeh (Lebanon)
- Vietnamese Pho (Vietnam)
- Egyptian Koshari (Egypt)
- Finnish Salmon Soup (Finland)
- Indonesian Nasi Goreng (Indonesia)
- Polish Pierogi (Poland)
- Belgian Waterzooi (Belgium)
- Cuban Ropa Vieja (Cuba)
- Portuguese Bacalhau à Brás (Portugal)
- Swiss Fondue (Switzerland)
- Peruvian Ceviche (Peru)
- Czech Goulash (Czech Republic)
- Dutch Stamppot (Netherlands)
- South African Bobotie (South Africa)
- Iranian Fesenjan (Iran)
- Hungarian Chicken Paprikash (Hungary)

- Filipino Adobo (Philippines)
- Canadian Tourtière (Canada)
- Australian Kangaroo Fillet (Australia)
- Jamaican Jerk Chicken (Jamaica)
- Nepalese Momos (Nepal)
- Georgian Khachapuri (Georgia)
- Burmese Mohinga (Myanmar)
- Chilean Pastel de Choclo (Chile)
- Danish Frikadeller (Denmark)
- Somali Sambusa (Somalia)
- Croatian Pasticada (Croatia)
- Israeli Shakshuka (Israel)
- Sri Lankan Kottu Roti (Sri Lanka)
- Venezuelan Arepas (Venezuela)
- Malaysian Laksa (Malaysia)

Coq au Vin

Ingredients:

- 1 whole chicken (about 4 lbs), cut into pieces
- 6 slices of bacon, diced
- 2 tablespoons olive oil
- 2 onions, chopped
- 2 carrots, sliced
- 4 cloves garlic, minced
- 2 cups red wine (preferably Burgundy)
- 1 cup chicken broth
- 2 tablespoons tomato paste
- 1 tablespoon flour
- 1 bouquet garni (parsley, thyme, bay leaf tied together)
- 10 pearl onions, peeled
- 8 ounces mushrooms, sliced
- Salt and pepper to taste
- Fresh parsley, chopped (for garnish)

Instructions:

1. **Prepare the Chicken:** Season the chicken pieces with salt and pepper. In a large Dutch oven or heavy pot, cook the bacon over medium heat until crisp. Remove with a slotted spoon and set aside.
2. **Brown the Chicken:** In the same pot, add the olive oil and brown the chicken pieces on all sides, working in batches if necessary. Once browned, remove the chicken and set aside.
3. **Sauté Vegetables:** Add the chopped onions, carrots, and garlic to the pot. Sauté until the onions are translucent, about 5-7 minutes.
4. **Deglaze:** Sprinkle the flour over the vegetables and stir to coat. Cook for 2-3 minutes, then add the tomato paste. Pour in the red wine and chicken broth, stirring to deglaze the pot. Bring to a simmer.
5. **Simmer the Chicken:** Return the chicken and bacon to the pot. Add the bouquet garni. Cover and simmer on low heat for about 1.5 hours, or until the chicken is tender.
6. **Prepare Garnishes:** While the chicken cooks, in a separate pan, sauté the pearl onions and mushrooms in a bit of butter or olive oil until golden brown. Set aside.

7. **Final Touch:** Once the chicken is tender, add the sautéed pearl onions and mushrooms to the pot. Simmer uncovered for another 10-15 minutes to thicken the sauce slightly.
8. **Serve:** Remove the bouquet garni. Garnish the dish with chopped fresh parsley before serving.

Paella Valenciana (Spain)

Ingredients:

- 1/4 cup olive oil
- 1 chicken, cut into pieces
- 1 rabbit (optional), cut into pieces
- 1 onion, chopped
- 2 tomatoes, chopped
- 1 bell pepper, chopped
- 3 cloves garlic, minced
- 1 1/2 cups short-grain rice (like Arborio)
- 4 cups chicken or seafood broth
- 1/2 teaspoon saffron threads
- 1/2 teaspoon paprika
- 1/2 cup peas
- 1/2 cup green beans, trimmed
- 1/2 cup artichoke hearts (optional)
- 1 lemon, cut into wedges
- Salt and pepper to taste

Instructions:

1. Heat olive oil in a large paella pan or wide skillet over medium heat. Brown the chicken and rabbit pieces (if using), and then remove and set aside.
2. Add onion, bell pepper, and garlic to the pan. Cook until softened.
3. Stir in chopped tomatoes, paprika, and saffron threads. Cook for 5 minutes until the tomatoes break down.
4. Add rice and stir to coat in the tomato mixture. Pour in the broth and bring to a boil.
5. Return the browned meat to the pan, then lower the heat and simmer for 20 minutes, adding peas, green beans, and artichokes in the last 10 minutes.
6. Cook until the liquid is absorbed and the rice is tender. Garnish with lemon wedges and serve.

Beef Wellington (United Kingdom)

Ingredients:

- 1 whole beef tenderloin (about 2 lbs)
- 2 tablespoons olive oil
- Salt and pepper to taste
- 2 tablespoons Dijon mustard
- 8 ounces mushrooms, finely chopped
- 1/2 cup pâté (optional)
- 1 sheet puff pastry
- 1 egg, beaten (for glazing)

Instructions:

1. Preheat oven to 400°F (200°C). Season beef tenderloin with salt and pepper, then sear on all sides in a hot pan with olive oil. Brush with Dijon mustard and let cool.
2. Sauté mushrooms in butter until moisture evaporates and they become a paste. Set aside to cool.
3. Roll out puff pastry and spread a thin layer of pâté (if using) over it. Spread mushroom mixture on top of the pâté, then place the beef on top.
4. Wrap the pastry around the beef, sealing the edges, and brush with beaten egg.
5. Bake for 25-30 minutes or until the pastry is golden and beef reaches desired doneness. Let rest before slicing.

Chicken Tikka Masala (India)

Ingredients:

- 2 chicken breasts, cubed
- 1/4 cup plain yogurt
- 2 tablespoons lemon juice
- 2 tablespoons garam masala
- 2 teaspoons ground cumin
- 1 teaspoon ground turmeric
- 1 teaspoon ground coriander
- 1 teaspoon paprika
- 1 tablespoon ginger, grated
- 2 tablespoons garlic, minced
- 1 onion, chopped
- 1 can (14 oz) diced tomatoes
- 1/2 cup heavy cream
- 2 tablespoons butter
- Salt and pepper to taste
- Fresh cilantro, chopped (for garnish)

Instructions:

1. Marinate chicken in yogurt, lemon juice, garam masala, cumin, turmeric, coriander, paprika, ginger, garlic, salt, and pepper. Let sit for at least 1 hour or overnight.
2. In a large skillet, melt butter and cook onions until soft. Add the marinated chicken and cook until browned on all sides.
3. Stir in tomatoes and simmer for 15 minutes until the chicken is cooked through.
4. Add cream and adjust seasoning with salt and pepper. Simmer for another 5 minutes.
5. Garnish with fresh cilantro and serve with rice or naan.

Szechuan Pork (China)

Ingredients:

- 1 lb pork tenderloin, thinly sliced
- 2 tablespoons soy sauce
- 1 tablespoon rice vinegar
- 2 tablespoons Szechuan peppercorns
- 1 tablespoon chili paste
- 3 cloves garlic, minced
- 1 tablespoon ginger, grated
- 1 bell pepper, sliced
- 1 onion, sliced
- 1/2 cup chicken broth
- 2 tablespoons vegetable oil
- Salt and pepper to taste

Instructions:

1. Marinate the pork in soy sauce and rice vinegar for 30 minutes.
2. Heat oil in a pan and toast the Szechuan peppercorns until fragrant. Add garlic, ginger, and chili paste, and sauté for a few minutes.
3. Add the pork slices and cook until browned. Remove and set aside.
4. Add the bell pepper and onion to the pan and cook until softened.
5. Return the pork to the pan and pour in the chicken broth. Stir to combine and simmer for 5-7 minutes.
6. Season with salt and pepper and serve hot with rice.

Sushi Rolls (Japan)

Ingredients:

- 2 cups sushi rice, cooked
- 2 tablespoons rice vinegar
- 1 tablespoon sugar
- 1/2 teaspoon salt
- 4 sheets nori (seaweed)
- 1/2 lb sushi-grade fish (salmon, tuna), sliced
- 1 cucumber, julienned
- 1 avocado, sliced
- Soy sauce, for serving
- Wasabi and pickled ginger, for serving

Instructions:

1. Mix rice vinegar, sugar, and salt in a small bowl. Stir into the cooked sushi rice and let it cool.
2. Place a sheet of nori on a bamboo sushi mat. Spread a thin layer of rice over the nori, leaving a 1-inch border at the top.
3. Arrange fish, cucumber, and avocado along the center of the rice.
4. Roll the sushi tightly, using the bamboo mat, then slice into pieces.
5. Serve with soy sauce, wasabi, and pickled ginger.

Osso Buco (Italy)

Ingredients:

- 4 veal shanks (with bone marrow)
- 2 tablespoons olive oil
- 1 onion, chopped
- 2 carrots, chopped
- 2 celery stalks, chopped
- 2 cloves garlic, minced
- 1 cup dry white wine
- 2 cups beef broth
- 1 can (14 oz) crushed tomatoes
- 2 sprigs thyme
- 1 bay leaf
- 1 tablespoon flour
- Salt and pepper to taste
- Gremolata (zest of 1 lemon, 2 tablespoons parsley, 1 garlic clove, minced)

Instructions:

1. Brown veal shanks in olive oil in a large pot. Remove and set aside.
2. Sauté onions, carrots, celery, and garlic until soft. Stir in flour and cook for 2 minutes.
3. Add wine to deglaze the pot, then stir in broth, tomatoes, thyme, and bay leaf.
4. Return veal to the pot, cover, and simmer for 2-3 hours until the meat is tender.
5. Garnish with gremolata and serve.

Moussaka (Greece)

Ingredients:

- 2 eggplants, sliced into rounds
- 1 lb ground lamb or beef
- 1 onion, chopped
- 2 cloves garlic, minced
- 1 can (14 oz) crushed tomatoes
- 1/2 cup red wine
- 1 teaspoon cinnamon
- 1/2 teaspoon nutmeg
- 1/4 cup flour
- 2 cups milk
- 1/4 cup grated Parmesan
- 1/4 cup butter
- 1 egg, beaten
- Salt and pepper to taste

Instructions:

1. Preheat oven to 375°F (190°C). Salt eggplant slices and let sit for 20 minutes to remove bitterness. Rinse and pat dry, then fry in olive oil until golden.
2. In a skillet, cook lamb or beef with onion and garlic until browned. Add tomatoes, wine, cinnamon, and nutmeg, and simmer for 20 minutes.
3. Make béchamel sauce: melt butter, stir in flour, and slowly add milk while whisking. Cook until thickened, then mix in Parmesan and beaten egg.
4. Layer eggplant, meat sauce, and béchamel in a baking dish. Bake for 45 minutes until golden and bubbling.

Korean Bibimbap (Korea)

Ingredients:

- 2 cups cooked rice
- 1/2 lb ground beef or pork
- 2 tablespoons soy sauce
- 1 tablespoon sesame oil
- 1 tablespoon sugar
- 1 teaspoon garlic, minced
- 1 carrot, julienned
- 1 cucumber, julienned
- 2 cups spinach, blanched
- 1 egg
- Gochujang (Korean chili paste)
- Sesame seeds for garnish

Instructions:

1. Sauté ground beef with soy sauce, sesame oil, sugar, and garlic until cooked.
2. Blanch spinach and sauté carrot and cucumber separately with a bit of sesame oil.
3. Fry an egg sunny-side up.
4. Assemble by placing rice in a bowl, topping with beef, vegetables, and a fried egg. Add a dollop of gochujang and sesame seeds. Mix before eating.

Moroccan Tagine (Morocco)

Ingredients:

- 2 tablespoons olive oil
- 1 lb chicken or lamb, cut into pieces
- 1 onion, chopped
- 2 cloves garlic, minced
- 1 teaspoon cumin
- 1 teaspoon turmeric
- 1 teaspoon cinnamon
- 1 can (14 oz) diced tomatoes
- 1/2 cup dried apricots, chopped
- 1/4 cup almonds
- 2 tablespoons honey
- Salt and pepper to taste
- Fresh cilantro for garnish

Instructions:

1. Heat olive oil in a tagine or pot and brown the meat. Remove and set aside.
2. Sauté onion and garlic, then add spices and cook for 2 minutes.
3. Add tomatoes, apricots, almonds, honey, and seasonings. Return meat to the pot and simmer for 1-2 hours.
4. Garnish with cilantro and serve with couscous.

Thai Green Curry (Thailand)

Ingredients:

- 1 tablespoon vegetable oil
- 1 lb chicken, sliced
- 1 can (14 oz) coconut milk
- 2 tablespoons green curry paste
- 1 tablespoon fish sauce
- 1 tablespoon brown sugar
- 1 bell pepper, sliced
- 1 zucchini, sliced
- 1/2 cup Thai basil leaves
- Rice for serving

Instructions:

1. Heat oil in a pot and cook chicken until browned.
2. Stir in curry paste and cook for 1 minute. Add coconut milk, fish sauce, and brown sugar, and bring to a simmer.
3. Add bell pepper, zucchini, and simmer for 10-15 minutes.
4. Garnish with Thai basil and serve with rice.

Turkish Manti (Turkey)

Ingredients:

- 2 cups flour
- 1 egg
- 1/2 cup water
- 1 lb ground beef or lamb
- 1 onion, finely chopped
- 1 teaspoon cumin
- Salt and pepper to taste
- Yogurt, for serving
- Butter, melted

Instructions:

1. Mix flour, egg, and water to form a dough. Roll out thinly and cut into squares.
2. Place a spoonful of meat mixture on each square, fold into triangles, and seal.
3. Boil manti in salted water until they float. Drain.
4. Serve with yogurt and melted butter.

Swedish Meatballs (Sweden)

Ingredients:

- 1 lb ground beef
- 1/2 lb ground pork
- 1/4 cup breadcrumbs
- 1/4 cup milk
- 1 egg
- 1/2 teaspoon allspice
- Salt and pepper to taste
- 2 tablespoons butter
- 1 cup beef broth
- 1/2 cup heavy cream

Instructions:

1. Mix meat, breadcrumbs, milk, egg, allspice, salt, and pepper. Form into small meatballs.
2. Brown meatballs in butter in a skillet, then remove and set aside.
3. Add beef broth and cream to the pan, stirring to combine. Return meatballs and simmer for 10-15 minutes.
4. Serve with mashed potatoes or lingonberry sauce.

Brazilian Feijoada (Brazil)

Ingredients:

- 1 lb pork shoulder, cubed
- 1/2 lb smoked sausage, sliced
- 1/2 lb chorizo, sliced
- 1 lb black beans, soaked overnight
- 1 onion, chopped
- 2 cloves garlic, minced
- 2 bay leaves
- 1 tablespoon cumin
- Salt and pepper to taste
- Orange slices for garnish

Instructions:

1. Brown pork shoulder, sausage, and chorizo in a large pot.
2. Add onion, garlic, and cook until softened. Stir in beans, bay leaves, and enough water to cover.
3. Simmer for 2-3 hours until beans are tender.
4. Season with salt and pepper and serve with rice and orange slices.

Ethiopian Doro Wat (Ethiopia)

Ingredients:

- 2 lbs chicken drumsticks or thighs
- 2 tablespoons niter kibbeh (spiced clarified butter)
- 1 large onion, chopped
- 4 cloves garlic, minced
- 1-inch piece of ginger, grated
- 1 tablespoon ground turmeric
- 1 tablespoon berbere spice mix
- 1 can (14 oz) crushed tomatoes
- 2 cups chicken broth
- 2 hard-boiled eggs, peeled
- Salt to taste
- Injera (for serving)

Instructions:

1. Heat niter kibbeh in a large pot, add onion, and cook until soft. Add garlic, ginger, turmeric, and berbere spice mix, cooking for another 2-3 minutes.
2. Stir in tomatoes and cook for 5 minutes. Add chicken and chicken broth. Simmer for 45 minutes, or until the chicken is tender.
3. Add the hard-boiled eggs and simmer for an additional 10 minutes.
4. Serve with injera.

Mexican Mole Poblano (Mexico)

Ingredients:

- 2 tablespoons vegetable oil
- 2 chicken breasts, skinless
- 1 onion, chopped
- 2 cloves garlic, minced
- 2 tablespoons cocoa powder
- 1 tablespoon sesame seeds
- 1 tablespoon chili powder
- 1 teaspoon cinnamon
- 1/2 teaspoon cumin
- 2 cups chicken broth
- 1 can (14 oz) diced tomatoes
- 1/4 cup almonds
- 1 tablespoon brown sugar
- Salt to taste

Instructions:

1. Heat oil in a pan and brown the chicken breasts on both sides. Remove and set aside.
2. In the same pan, sauté onion and garlic until soft. Add cocoa powder, sesame seeds, chili powder, cinnamon, and cumin. Cook for 2 minutes.
3. Add chicken broth, diced tomatoes, almonds, and brown sugar. Simmer for 15 minutes.
4. Blend the sauce until smooth. Return the chicken to the pan and simmer for another 20 minutes.
5. Serve with rice.

Russian Beef Stroganoff (Russia)

Ingredients:

- 1 lb beef tenderloin, sliced into strips
- 2 tablespoons butter
- 1 onion, chopped
- 2 cloves garlic, minced
- 1 cup mushrooms, sliced
- 1 cup beef broth
- 1 tablespoon Dijon mustard
- 1/2 cup sour cream
- 2 tablespoons flour
- Salt and pepper to taste

Instructions:

1. In a skillet, melt butter and cook beef strips until browned. Remove and set aside.
2. Add onion, garlic, and mushrooms to the skillet and sauté until soft.
3. Sprinkle flour over the vegetables and cook for 2 minutes. Stir in beef broth and mustard. Simmer for 5 minutes.
4. Add sour cream, return beef to the pan, and cook for another 5 minutes.
5. Season with salt and pepper and serve with egg noodles.

German Sauerbraten (Germany)

Ingredients:

- 3 lb beef roast (preferably chuck)
- 2 onions, chopped
- 1 cup vinegar
- 2 cups beef broth
- 2 tablespoons sugar
- 2 teaspoons ginger, grated
- 1 tablespoon mustard seeds
- 2 bay leaves
- Salt and pepper to taste

Instructions:

1. In a large bowl, mix vinegar, broth, sugar, ginger, mustard seeds, bay leaves, and salt. Add beef and marinate for 2-3 days.
2. Remove the beef from the marinade and sear on all sides in a hot pan.
3. Add onions and the marinade to the pot, bringing it to a boil. Simmer for 2-3 hours, until the meat is tender.
4. Remove the beef, thicken the sauce with a cornstarch slurry, and serve with mashed potatoes.

Argentinian Asado (Argentina)

Ingredients:

- 2 lbs beef ribs
- 1 tablespoon olive oil
- 1 tablespoon garlic, minced
- 1 tablespoon rosemary, chopped
- 1 teaspoon paprika
- Salt and pepper to taste
- Chimichurri sauce (for serving)

Instructions:

1. Preheat the grill (parrilla) or oven to medium-high heat.
2. Rub the beef ribs with olive oil, garlic, rosemary, paprika, salt, and pepper.
3. Grill the ribs for about 1.5 to 2 hours, turning occasionally, until cooked to your desired level of doneness.
4. Serve with chimichurri sauce.

Lebanese Kibbeh (Lebanon)

Ingredients:

- 1 lb ground lamb or beef
- 1 cup bulgur wheat
- 1 onion, chopped
- 2 teaspoons cinnamon
- 1 teaspoon allspice
- 1/2 teaspoon cumin
- 1/4 cup pine nuts
- 1/4 cup parsley, chopped
- Salt and pepper to taste
- Olive oil for frying

Instructions:

1. Soak the bulgur in water for 30 minutes, then drain. Combine with ground meat, onions, spices, and salt.
2. Shape the mixture into oval patties, then make an indentation to stuff with pine nuts and parsley.
3. Seal the patties and fry in olive oil until golden brown.
4. Serve with yogurt.

Vietnamese Pho (Vietnam)

Ingredients:

- 1 lb beef brisket, thinly sliced
- 1 onion, halved
- 2-inch piece of ginger, sliced
- 2 star anise
- 1 cinnamon stick
- 1 tablespoon coriander seeds
- 4 cups beef broth
- 1 tablespoon fish sauce
- 1 tablespoon soy sauce
- 1 package rice noodles
- Fresh basil, cilantro, lime wedges, and bean sprouts (for garnish)

Instructions:

1. In a large pot, toast star anise, cinnamon, and coriander seeds. Add beef broth, onion, ginger, fish sauce, and soy sauce. Simmer for 1 hour.
2. Cook rice noodles according to package instructions.
3. Strain the broth and return it to the pot. Add thinly sliced beef and cook for 2-3 minutes.
4. Serve the broth over noodles and garnish with basil, cilantro, lime wedges, and bean sprouts.

Egyptian Koshari (Egypt)

Ingredients:

- 1 cup rice
- 1/2 cup lentils
- 1/2 cup macaroni
- 1 onion, chopped
- 3 cloves garlic, minced
- 2 cups tomato sauce
- 1 teaspoon cumin
- 1 tablespoon vinegar
- 1 tablespoon olive oil
- Salt and pepper to taste

Instructions:

1. Cook rice, lentils, and macaroni separately.
2. In a pan, heat olive oil and sauté onion and garlic until golden.
3. Stir in tomato sauce, cumin, vinegar, salt, and pepper. Simmer for 10 minutes.
4. Layer rice, lentils, and macaroni in a serving dish. Top with tomato sauce mixture and fried onions.
5. Serve warm.

Finnish Salmon Soup (Finland)

Ingredients:

- 1 lb salmon fillet, cubed
- 4 cups vegetable broth
- 2 potatoes, diced
- 1 onion, chopped
- 2 carrots, sliced
- 1 cup heavy cream
- 1 tablespoon dill, chopped
- Salt and pepper to taste

Instructions:

1. In a pot, cook onion, carrots, and potatoes in vegetable broth until tender.
2. Add salmon cubes and cook for 10 minutes.
3. Stir in heavy cream and dill. Simmer for another 5 minutes.
4. Season with salt and pepper, and serve hot.

Indonesian Nasi Goreng (Indonesia)

Ingredients:

- 2 cups cooked jasmine rice (preferably cold)
- 2 tablespoons vegetable oil
- 2 cloves garlic, minced
- 1 onion, chopped
- 1 red chili, chopped (optional)
- 2 eggs, beaten
- 1/4 cup sweet soy sauce (kecap manis)
- 1 tablespoon soy sauce
- 1/2 cup cooked chicken, shredded
- 1/2 cup shrimp, peeled and deveined (optional)
- 1/4 cup peas (optional)
- Fresh cilantro, chopped (for garnish)

Instructions:

1. Heat oil in a wok or large pan. Add garlic, onion, and chili (if using) and sauté until softened.
2. Push the ingredients to the side and scramble the eggs in the same pan.
3. Add the cold rice to the pan, breaking up any clumps. Stir-fry for a few minutes.
4. Stir in the soy sauces, chicken, shrimp, peas, and mix well.
5. Serve garnished with fresh cilantro.

Polish Pierogi (Poland)

Ingredients:

- 2 cups all-purpose flour
- 1/2 teaspoon salt
- 1 large egg
- 1/2 cup sour cream
- 1/4 cup butter, melted
- 2 cups mashed potatoes
- 1 cup cheese (cheddar or farmer's cheese), shredded
- Salt and pepper to taste
- Butter, for frying

Instructions:

1. Combine flour, salt, egg, sour cream, and melted butter. Mix until smooth. Knead until dough is soft. Cover and let rest.
2. Roll dough out and cut into circles. Spoon mashed potatoes and cheese into the center of each circle.
3. Fold dough over and seal edges by pinching or pressing with a fork.
4. Boil pierogi in salted water until they float, about 5 minutes.
5. For a crispy texture, fry boiled pierogi in butter until golden brown.

Belgian Waterzooi (Belgium)

Ingredients:

- 4 chicken breasts, bone-in or boneless
- 4 cups chicken broth
- 2 carrots, chopped
- 2 potatoes, chopped
- 1 onion, chopped
- 2 cloves garlic, minced
- 1 cup heavy cream
- 2 egg yolks
- Salt and pepper to taste
- Fresh parsley, chopped (for garnish)

Instructions:

1. Boil chicken in broth with carrots, potatoes, onion, and garlic until tender, about 45 minutes.
2. Remove chicken and shred it. Return chicken to the pot.
3. In a bowl, whisk egg yolks and cream. Slowly stir this mixture into the pot and cook over low heat for 10 minutes, stirring constantly.
4. Season with salt and pepper, and garnish with fresh parsley before serving.

Cuban Ropa Vieja (Cuba)

Ingredients:

- 2 lbs flank steak
- 1 onion, sliced
- 1 bell pepper, sliced
- 3 cloves garlic, minced
- 1 can (14 oz) diced tomatoes
- 1/4 cup dry white wine
- 1/4 cup green olives, pitted and chopped
- 1 tablespoon capers
- 1 teaspoon cumin
- 1 teaspoon oregano
- 1 bay leaf
- Salt and pepper to taste

Instructions:

1. Brown the flank steak in a hot pan, then simmer it in water for about 2 hours until tender.
2. Shred the beef into strips.
3. In the same pan, sauté onions, bell peppers, and garlic until softened.
4. Stir in tomatoes, white wine, olives, capers, cumin, oregano, bay leaf, and seasonings.
5. Add the shredded beef and simmer for 30 minutes, allowing flavors to meld.

Portuguese Bacalhau à Brás (Portugal)

Ingredients:

- 1 lb salted cod (bacalhau), soaked overnight
- 1 onion, chopped
- 4 cloves garlic, minced
- 1/4 cup olive oil
- 4 large potatoes, julienned and fried
- 6 eggs, beaten
- 1/4 cup parsley, chopped
- Salt and pepper to taste

Instructions:

1. Rinse the cod and cook it in water for 15 minutes. Shred the fish and set aside.
2. Heat olive oil and sauté onion and garlic until softened.
3. Add the shredded cod and fried potatoes. Stir in beaten eggs, and cook until eggs are set.
4. Season with salt, pepper, and garnish with parsley.

Swiss Fondue (Switzerland)

Ingredients:

- 1 lb Gruyère cheese, shredded
- 1 lb Emmental cheese, shredded
- 2 tablespoons cornstarch
- 1 1/2 cups dry white wine
- 1 clove garlic, halved
- 1 tablespoon lemon juice
- 1/4 teaspoon nutmeg
- Freshly ground black pepper
- French bread cubes (for dipping)

Instructions:

1. Toss the cheese with cornstarch and set aside.
2. Rub the inside of a fondue pot with garlic, then add wine and lemon juice. Heat gently.
3. Gradually add cheese, stirring constantly, until smooth.
4. Season with nutmeg and pepper.
5. Serve with French bread cubes for dipping.

Peruvian Ceviche (Peru)

Ingredients:

- 1 lb fresh fish fillets (such as tilapia or snapper), diced
- 1 red onion, thinly sliced
- 1-2 serrano chilis, chopped
- 1 cup fresh lime juice
- 1/4 cup fresh cilantro, chopped
- Salt and pepper to taste

Instructions:

1. Mix fish, onion, and chili in a bowl.
2. Pour lime juice over the mixture and let it marinate in the refrigerator for 2-3 hours.
3. Stir in cilantro and season with salt and pepper.
4. Serve chilled with crackers or corn.

Czech Goulash (Czech Republic)

Ingredients:

- 2 lbs beef stew meat, cubed
- 1 onion, chopped
- 2 tablespoons paprika
- 2 cloves garlic, minced
- 1 can (14 oz) crushed tomatoes
- 1 cup beef broth
- 1 tablespoon caraway seeds
- Salt and pepper to taste
- Dumplings or bread (for serving)

Instructions:

1. Brown the beef cubes in a large pot. Remove and set aside.
2. In the same pot, sauté onions, garlic, and paprika.
3. Add beef broth, tomatoes, caraway seeds, and beef. Simmer for 1.5 hours until beef is tender.
4. Season with salt and pepper and serve with dumplings or bread.

Dutch Stamppot (Netherlands)

Ingredients:

- 2 lbs potatoes, peeled and diced
- 1 lb kale or sauerkraut
- 1 onion, chopped
- 2 tablespoons butter
- 1/2 cup milk
- Salt and pepper to taste
- Smoked sausage (for serving)

Instructions:

1. Boil potatoes until tender. In a separate pot, cook kale or sauerkraut with the onion.
2. Mash the potatoes with butter and milk, then stir in the kale or sauerkraut mixture.
3. Season with salt and pepper.
4. Serve with smoked sausage on top.

South African Bobotie (South Africa)

Ingredients:

- 1 lb ground beef or lamb
- 2 tablespoons vegetable oil
- 1 onion, chopped
- 2 cloves garlic, minced
- 1 tablespoon curry powder
- 1/2 teaspoon turmeric
- 1/2 cup breadcrumbs
- 1/4 cup raisins
- 1/4 cup almonds, chopped
- 2 tablespoons chutney
- 1/4 cup milk
- 2 eggs
- Salt and pepper to taste
- Fresh parsley, chopped (for garnish)

Instructions:

1. Heat oil and sauté onions and garlic until softened. Add ground meat and cook until browned.
2. Stir in curry powder, turmeric, breadcrumbs, raisins, almonds, and chutney.
3. In a separate bowl, whisk together milk and eggs, then pour over the meat mixture.
4. Bake in a preheated oven at 350°F for 30 minutes, until the top is set and golden brown.
5. Garnish with fresh parsley before serving.

Iranian Fesenjan (Iran)

Ingredients:

- 2 lbs chicken thighs or duck, bone-in
- 2 tablespoons vegetable oil
- 1 onion, chopped
- 1 cup pomegranate molasses
- 1/2 cup ground walnuts
- 1 tablespoon sugar
- 1/4 teaspoon cinnamon
- 1/4 teaspoon turmeric
- Salt and pepper to taste
- 2 cups chicken broth

Instructions:

1. Brown the chicken in oil and set aside.
2. In the same pot, sauté onion until softened. Add turmeric, cinnamon, and ground walnuts, stirring for a minute.
3. Add pomegranate molasses, sugar, chicken broth, and chicken pieces to the pot. Simmer for 45 minutes, or until the chicken is tender.
4. Season with salt and pepper before serving.

Hungarian Chicken Paprikash (Hungary)

Ingredients:

- 2 lbs chicken thighs or drumsticks
- 2 tablespoons vegetable oil
- 1 onion, chopped
- 2 cloves garlic, minced
- 2 tablespoons sweet paprika
- 1 teaspoon hot paprika (optional)
- 1 cup chicken broth
- 1 cup sour cream
- Salt and pepper to taste

Instructions:

1. Brown the chicken in oil, then remove and set aside.
2. In the same pan, sauté onions and garlic until softened. Add paprika and stir to coat.
3. Return the chicken to the pan and add chicken broth. Simmer for 30 minutes, or until chicken is tender.
4. Stir in sour cream and season with salt and pepper.
5. Serve with dumplings or rice.

Filipino Adobo (Philippines)

Ingredients:

- 2 lbs chicken or pork, cut into pieces
- 1/4 cup soy sauce
- 1/4 cup vinegar
- 1 onion, chopped
- 4 cloves garlic, minced
- 2 bay leaves
- 1 teaspoon peppercorns
- 1 tablespoon brown sugar
- 1 cup water
- Salt and pepper to taste

Instructions:

1. In a bowl, combine soy sauce, vinegar, garlic, onions, bay leaves, and peppercorns. Marinate the meat for at least 30 minutes.
2. In a pot, cook the marinated meat with the marinade, sugar, and water. Simmer for 40 minutes, or until tender.
3. Season with salt and pepper before serving.

Canadian Tourtière (Canada)

Ingredients:

- 1 lb ground pork
- 1 lb ground beef
- 1 onion, chopped
- 1/2 teaspoon ground cinnamon
- 1/2 teaspoon ground cloves
- 1/2 teaspoon ground allspice
- 1/2 teaspoon thyme
- 1/2 cup beef broth
- 1/4 cup breadcrumbs
- 1 package pie crusts (or homemade)
- Salt and pepper to taste

Instructions:

1. Brown the meat with onions in a pan. Add cinnamon, cloves, allspice, and thyme.
2. Stir in beef broth and simmer until liquid is reduced. Mix in breadcrumbs to thicken.
3. Preheat oven to 375°F. Place meat mixture into the pie crust, cover with the second crust, and seal edges.
4. Bake for 40 minutes or until golden brown. Serve hot.

Australian Kangaroo Fillet (Australia)

Ingredients:

- 2 kangaroo fillets
- 2 tablespoons olive oil
- 2 cloves garlic, minced
- 1 teaspoon fresh rosemary, chopped
- Salt and pepper to taste

Instructions:

1. Heat olive oil in a pan. Season fillets with garlic, rosemary, salt, and pepper.
2. Sear the fillets for 3-4 minutes per side, depending on thickness.
3. Let rest for a few minutes before slicing and serving.

Jamaican Jerk Chicken (Jamaica)

Ingredients:

- 4 chicken thighs or drumsticks
- 2 tablespoons jerk seasoning
- 1/4 cup olive oil
- 1 lime, juiced
- 2 cloves garlic, minced
- 1 teaspoon fresh thyme, chopped
- Salt and pepper to taste

Instructions:

1. Marinate the chicken with jerk seasoning, lime juice, garlic, thyme, olive oil, salt, and pepper for at least 2 hours.
2. Grill the chicken over medium heat for 20-25 minutes, turning occasionally, until fully cooked.
3. Serve with rice and peas.

Nepalese Momos (Nepal)

Ingredients:

- 1 lb ground chicken or pork
- 1 onion, finely chopped
- 2 cloves garlic, minced
- 1 tablespoon ginger, minced
- 2 tablespoons soy sauce
- 1/4 teaspoon cumin
- 1/4 teaspoon coriander
- 1 teaspoon fresh cilantro, chopped
- 1 package dumpling wrappers

Instructions:

1. Mix ground meat, onion, garlic, ginger, soy sauce, cumin, coriander, and cilantro.
2. Place a small spoonful of filling in the center of each dumpling wrapper. Fold and seal edges.
3. Steam the momos for 15-20 minutes, or until the dough is translucent.
4. Serve with dipping sauce.

Georgian Khachapuri (Georgia)

Ingredients:

- 2 cups all-purpose flour
- 1/2 teaspoon salt
- 2 teaspoons sugar
- 1 packet active dry yeast
- 3/4 cup warm water
- 1 tablespoon olive oil
- 1 1/2 cups mozzarella cheese, shredded
- 1/2 cup feta cheese, crumbled
- 1 egg (for topping)

Instructions:

1. Combine flour, salt, sugar, yeast, and warm water. Knead into dough and let rise for 1 hour.
2. Preheat oven to 400°F. Roll out dough into an oval shape and place on a baking sheet.
3. Mix cheeses and fill the center of the dough, leaving edges uncovered.
4. Bake for 15-20 minutes until golden, then crack an egg into the center and return to the oven for 5 more minutes.
5. Serve hot.

Burmese Mohinga (Myanmar)

Ingredients:

- 1 lb fish fillets (catfish or tilapia), boneless and skinless
- 2 tablespoons vegetable oil
- 2 stalks lemongrass, chopped
- 3 cloves garlic, minced
- 1-inch piece ginger, minced
- 1 onion, chopped
- 4 cups fish stock
- 2 tablespoons fish sauce
- 1 tablespoon turmeric
- 1 teaspoon chili powder
- 2 tablespoons rice noodles, cooked
- Fresh cilantro, chopped (for garnish)

Instructions:

1. Cook fish in a pot of water for 10-15 minutes until tender. Remove and shred the fish.
2. Heat oil in a pot and sauté garlic, ginger, onion, and lemongrass until fragrant.
3. Add fish stock, fish sauce, turmeric, and chili powder. Simmer for 20 minutes.
4. Add shredded fish and noodles to the broth. Garnish with fresh cilantro before serving.

Chilean Pastel de Choclo (Chile)

Ingredients:

- 2 cups fresh corn kernels (or frozen)
- 1 lb ground beef
- 1 onion, chopped
- 2 cloves garlic, minced
- 1/2 cup black olives, chopped
- 2 boiled eggs, chopped
- 1/4 cup raisins
- 1 tablespoon sugar
- 1/4 teaspoon cumin
- 1 tablespoon paprika
- 1/2 cup milk
- 2 tablespoons butter
- Salt and pepper to taste

Instructions:

1. Cook the corn kernels in a pot until soft. Blend with milk and butter to create a creamy mixture.
2. Brown the ground beef with onions, garlic, cumin, paprika, and raisins. Add olives and boiled eggs.
3. Preheat oven to 375°F. In a baking dish, layer the beef mixture, then spread the corn mixture over the top.
4. Bake for 20-25 minutes until the top is golden.
5. Serve hot.

Danish Frikadeller (Denmark)

Ingredients:

- 1 lb ground pork (or a mix of pork and beef)
- 1/2 cup breadcrumbs
- 1/4 cup milk
- 1 onion, finely chopped
- 1 egg
- 1 teaspoon salt
- 1/4 teaspoon black pepper
- 2 tablespoons butter for frying

Instructions:

1. Soak the breadcrumbs in milk and set aside.
2. In a bowl, combine ground meat, soaked breadcrumbs, onion, egg, salt, and pepper.
3. Shape into small patties.
4. Fry in butter over medium heat for 5-7 minutes on each side until golden brown.
5. Serve with potatoes and pickled vegetables.

Somali Sambusa (Somalia)

Ingredients:

- 1 lb ground beef or lamb
- 1 onion, chopped
- 1/4 cup cilantro, chopped
- 1 teaspoon cumin
- 1 teaspoon turmeric
- 1/2 teaspoon cinnamon
- 1 tablespoon vegetable oil
- 1 package spring roll wrappers
- Salt and pepper to taste

Instructions:

1. Sauté onion and ground meat in oil until browned. Add spices, cilantro, salt, and pepper.
2. Cool the filling before placing a spoonful in each spring roll wrapper.
3. Fold and seal the wrappers, then fry the sambusas in hot oil until golden brown.
4. Drain on paper towels and serve with a dipping sauce.

Croatian Pasticada (Croatia)

Ingredients:

- 2 lbs beef chuck, cut into large chunks
- 1 onion, chopped
- 2 cloves garlic, minced
- 2 tablespoons olive oil
- 1 cup red wine
- 1/2 cup beef broth
- 2 tablespoons tomato paste
- 1 tablespoon brown sugar
- 1 teaspoon dried thyme
- 2 bay leaves
- Salt and pepper to taste

Instructions:

1. Brown beef chunks in olive oil and set aside. Sauté onions and garlic in the same pan.
2. Add tomato paste, wine, beef broth, sugar, thyme, bay leaves, salt, and pepper.
3. Return beef to the pan, cover, and simmer for 2-3 hours until tender.
4. Serve with gnocchi or mashed potatoes.

Israeli Shakshuka (Israel)

Ingredients:

- 2 tablespoons olive oil
- 1 onion, chopped
- 1 bell pepper, chopped
- 4 tomatoes, chopped
- 2 teaspoons ground cumin
- 1/2 teaspoon paprika
- 4 eggs
- Salt and pepper to taste
- Fresh parsley, chopped (for garnish)

Instructions:

1. Heat olive oil in a pan and sauté onions and bell pepper until softened.
2. Add tomatoes, cumin, paprika, salt, and pepper. Simmer for 10-15 minutes.
3. Make small wells in the sauce and crack eggs into them.
4. Cover and cook for 5-7 minutes, until the eggs are done to your liking.
5. Garnish with fresh parsley and serve with pita.

Sri Lankan Kottu Roti (Sri Lanka)

Ingredients:

- 2 cups shredded roti (or flatbread)
- 1/2 lb chicken, cooked and shredded
- 1 onion, chopped
- 2 cloves garlic, minced
- 2 carrots, julienned
- 2 eggs, beaten
- 2 tablespoons soy sauce
- 1 tablespoon curry powder
- 1/2 teaspoon turmeric
- Salt and pepper to taste
- 2 tablespoons vegetable oil

Instructions:

1. Heat oil in a large pan and sauté onion, garlic, and carrots.
2. Add shredded chicken, curry powder, turmeric, soy sauce, and cook for a few minutes.
3. Push the mixture to one side and scramble the eggs in the same pan.
4. Add shredded roti and mix everything together. Cook for 5 minutes.
5. Serve hot with extra soy sauce.

Venezuelan Arepas (Venezuela)

Ingredients:

- 2 cups arepa flour (masarepa)
- 1 1/2 cups warm water
- 1 teaspoon salt
- 1 tablespoon vegetable oil

Instructions:

1. Combine the arepa flour, water, salt, and oil in a bowl. Mix until a dough forms.
2. Divide the dough into small balls and flatten into discs.
3. Cook the arepas on a griddle over medium heat for 5-7 minutes per side until golden and slightly crisp.
4. Split open and stuff with cheese, meat, or other fillings as desired.

Malaysian Laksa (Malaysia)

Ingredients:

- 1 lb shrimp, peeled and deveined
- 2 tablespoons vegetable oil
- 1 onion, chopped
- 2 cloves garlic, minced
- 1-inch piece ginger, minced
- 2 tablespoons red curry paste
- 2 cups coconut milk
- 4 cups chicken broth
- 2 tablespoons fish sauce
- 200g rice noodles
- 2 boiled eggs, halved
- Fresh cilantro and lime wedges for garnish

Instructions:

1. Sauté onions, garlic, ginger, and curry paste in oil until fragrant.
2. Add coconut milk, chicken broth, fish sauce, and bring to a boil.
3. Cook the shrimp in the broth for 3-4 minutes, then remove and set aside.
4. Cook the noodles according to package instructions and divide into bowls.
5. Pour soup over the noodles, add shrimp, boiled eggs, cilantro, and lime wedges for garnish. Serve hot.